# Watch Out This Tro Shouts:

T0337559

Written by Emily Hibbs

Illustrated by Karl West

## Collins

Troll's cave was huge and gloomy.
The walls were splodged with slime.

Troll's cave had a special stink.
The ground was thick with grime.

Creatures walked by the bridge outside,
but no one ever drew near.
"I know," thought Troll, "I'll shout at them,
then they'll know I'm here."

On Monday, Gnome plodded past, singing a cheery tune.

"What is that atrocious noise?" a voice roared from the gloom.

"Sounds like a goat with a croaky throat,"
Troll sneered (but it wasn't true).

Gnome's voice was sweet and crystal clear,
but sneering was something to do.

On Tuesday, Unicorn neighed nearby.
His designer hooves were flashing.

His coarse mane had been curled and combed.
He felt fabulously dashing!

"What a silly sight!" Troll jeered.
"You look totally absurd!"

He knew that Unicorn looked great,
but shouting made him feel heard.

The next day all was quiet,
until Knight strode straight by.

He was peering at a poem
and the message made him cry.

"Why so emotional, big man?"
taunted Troll from his grey cave.

"You're bawling like a baby –
aren't knights meant to be brave?"

On Thursday, Troll mocked
Howl's knitting.

(On Friday, he took a break.)

On Saturday, he yelled at Witch,
"Your potion powers are fake!"

Outside the cave on Sunday,
Princess practised karate kicks.

She jumped, she spun, she struck ...
and a large tree fell with two flicks!

"Ha! That was rubbish!" Troll roared.
His voice surged far and wide.

"Princesses can't do martial arts –
it's embarrassing you tried!"

It was a great week of shouting,
even if Troll's throat felt sore.

He couldn't wait until next week,
when he could shout some more.

But no one trudged by on Monday.
Tuesday was quiet, too.

Nobody crossed the bridge all week.
Troll soon ran out of things to do.

At night, Troll climbed into bed
and stared numbly into space.

All the naughty things he'd shouted
couldn't fill that empty place.

Then, one morning, he saw Princess
put a sign up by the stream.

It said:

Watch out:

this troll shouts!
(and what he shouts
is mean!)

Then Princess caught sight of Troll.
Her words came pouring out:

"You're mean to all who cross your bridge.
Why do you always shout?"

Watch out:

this troll shouts!
(and what he shouts
is mean!)

Troll peered sadly at the sign.
He asked, "Is that what you see?

All I did was shout some things
so that you would notice me."

"Well, Gnome won't sing," said Princess.
"Unicorn can't leave his stall.

Howl and Witch are over it,
but you made Knight feel so small."

As Princess spoke, Troll listened,
and heard what his words had done.

Suddenly, sneering from the dark
didn't seem quite so much fun.

"Those jeers were just for fun," Troll said.
"I didn't know they'd sting!

Now I've been taught, I feel distraught
and wish I'd not said a thing!"

Troll crossed the bridge to the village –
at last he understood.

He was ready to be kinder.
It was time to do some good!

First, he knocked on Gnome's door
and said a little gruffly,

"I'm sorry for what I shouted –
your voice is really lovely."

Next, he said to Unicorn, "I shouldn't have judged or told lies."

"I adore your rainbow mane. The colours bring out your eyes."

In Knight's mansion, Troll declared,
"I'm sorry – it's good to cry.

I've never read a book like yours.
Perhaps I should give one a try."

Now that he'd said sorry,
Troll knew he had to be brave.

"I promise it's now my mission
to shout nice things from my cave."

"Not so fast!" the creatures cried.
"Don't go back to that grim, grey place.

Instead of shouting from the dark,
why don't we talk face-to-face?"

# Troll's diary

Monday    Tuesday    ~~Wednesday~~    Thursday

Friday    Saturday    Sunday

**Day off !**

Notes

Great week for shouting !

Monday   Tuesday      Thursday

Friday   Saturday   Sunday

**Said sorry.**

# ☙ Review: After reading ☙

Use your assessment from hearing the children read to choose any GPCs, words or tricky words that need additional practice.

## Read 1: Decoding

- Ask the children to find the following words and to read the words or sentences around them to work out their meaning:
  - Page 4: **atrocious** – ask: What is an "atrocious noise"? (e.g. *a horrible/awful noise*)
  - Page 5: **crystal** – ask: What would a "crystal clear" voice be like? (e.g. *a bright voice that is easy to hear – like a glassy bright crystal*)
- Challenge the children to take turns to read a sentence, sounding out and blending in their heads. Suggest they break longer words into chunks to help them, for example: **em/barr/ass/ing**.

## Read 2: Prosody

- Ask the children to work in groups of three to prepare a dramatic reading of pages 14 and 15, with the children reading the parts of the narrator (and sign), the Princess and the Troll.
- Encourage the narrator to use a cross voice for the sign; the Princess to sound angry and upset; the Troll to feel embarrassed and sad.
- Let the children read their pages to the class, and encourage positive feedback.

## Read 3: Comprehension

- Ask the children if they have read any other stories about trolls. Ask: What was the character of the troll like? Remind the children of the story *Three Billy Goats Gruff* and ask if they are familiar with it.
- Discuss the ending of the story. Ask: Did Troll learn a lesson? Return to pages 15 to 17 if necessary, and point out the effects of Troll being naughty.
- Turn to pages 22 and 23 and allocate one of the pictures (and the day of the week) to a child or small group of children. Explain that you want them to prepare to retell their part of the story:
  - Look up what happened or make it up.
  - Decide what happened and what the character or characters said/shouted.
  - Let the children tell the story in order.